*This Time...*

## Acknowledgement

Some poems in this volume previously appeared in *Waterlines*,
an anthology published by *Three Pines Publishing (2010)*.

*Fly Boy, Fly, Say it Plain, In the Cemetery,
Don't Just Stand There—Scream! Run!,
Prayer of the Cockroach, My Choice.*

*Did She Carry Him Because He Was Old?* appeared in *Waterlines*,
after first appearing in *Dunes Review, vol. 15, Issue I,* Summer 2010.

**Photography Credits**
Page 11, "Walking the Same Way," *Julie DeNooyer*
Page 77, "Moonlight on Lake," *Tom Speet*
Page 86, "Trail," *David Randall*
Page 107, "Winter Has Come," *Linda Avery*
Cover & pages 4, 22, 29, 42, 57, 64, 82, 112 – shutterstock.com

Cover & book design by Quinn Steendam Design, LLC
citrusdesignstudio@gmail.com
Rockford, Michigan, USA

# This Time...

## Colette Volkema DeNooyer

*Poems*

Chapbook Press

Schuler Books
2660 28th Street SE
Grand Rapids, MI 49512
(616) 942-7330
www.schulerbooks.com

This Time.... Poems

ISBN 13: 9781943359479

eBook ISBN: 9781966196044

Library of Congress Control Number: 2016958547

Copyright © 2016, Colette Volkema DeNooyer

All rights reserved.

No part of this book may be reproduced in any form without express permission of the copyright holder.

**Printed in the United States by Chapbook Press.**

*for Bob — who smiles whenever I am writing*

*for Nicole and Chris, Colin and Wyatt
Dominique and Julie, Jacob and Ethan and Alex —
so you will always know*

*and for Jack Ridl —
ever and always inspiration, mentor & friend*

*Just this little time and
perhaps a little more*

  – Jack Ridl, *from Suite for the Turning of the Year*

On Writing .................................................................................................... *i*

## The Birds Are Singing Again

Quiet Quiet Now ........................................................................................... 1
I Am Small ..................................................................................................... 3
The Birds Are Singing Again ...................................................................... 5
Dessert Always Tastes Better When You Eat It First ................................ 6
Morning Prayer ............................................................................................. 9
They Walk the Same Way .......................................................................... 10
Write a Poem ............................................................................................... 13
It Could Have Been Otherwise ................................................................. 15
In the Cemetery .......................................................................................... 17
Ode to Change ............................................................................................ 19
Fly Boy Fly ................................................................................................... 21
Keep Going This Way ................................................................................ 23
When You Feel That Old Fear Coming Towards You,
Here's What You Do .................................................................................. 24
Prayer of the Cockroach ............................................................................ 27
Walking the Beach ..................................................................................... 28
My Choice .................................................................................................... 31
Valentine ...................................................................................................... 33
When You Have Nothing to Say ............................................................... 35

## Through the Fog

The Trajectory ............................................................................................ 39
Tell Me .......................................................................................................... 41
This Time ..................................................................................................... 43
News, Sports and Weather ........................................................................ 44
Through the Fog ......................................................................................... 47

I Didn't Know ........................................................................................ *49*
Did She Carry Him Because He Was Old? ...................................... *51*
Now and Then ..................................................................................... *53*
What If God Is Praying to Us? ........................................................... *55*
Poem I Don't Want Read on My 80th Birthday .............................. *56*
Gone the Sun ........................................................................................ *59*
There Is Nothing You Can Do ........................................................... *61*
This One Is for You .............................................................................. *63*
Counting ............................................................................................... *65*
Don't Just Stand There — Scream! Run! .......................................... *67*
On Seeing Again — My Father's Face .............................................. *69*
Put Down Your Pack ........................................................................... *70*
Say It Plain ............................................................................................ *73*
The Sea .................................................................................................. *75*
Let the Poem Come to You ................................................................ *76*

## In My Time Capsule

Little Man ............................................................................................. *81*
Remembering Seagulls ....................................................................... *83*
Bread and Wine ................................................................................... *85*
After Words .......................................................................................... *87*
Morning Sky ......................................................................................... *89*
Life after Forty ..................................................................................... *91*
For My Son at Thirty-Two ................................................................. *93*
In Your Time Capsule ......................................................................... *95*
The Dancer ........................................................................................... *97*
The Two of You ................................................................................... *99*
"This Snow is Delicious" .................................................................... *100*
You Did Not Want to Stay ................................................................. *102*
On Your Birthday ................................................................................ *105*
Summer Is Almost Over ..................................................................... *106*
In My Time Capsule ............................................................................ *108*
Star Light .............................................................................................. *111*

*End Notes* ............................................................................................. *113*

# On Writing

See what the morning gives you,
what seeps in from the day
before. Say something about
the regret, what you said
that you would take back now
if you could. Though
you never can. Or mention
that moment when you
*stayed* with the colors
splayed across the western sky,
the magic show of sundown, clouds
grey and white turning yellow gold,
orange, fire roasted red. Say you were
satisfied — no small miracle that.
Felt no urge to rearrange the
clouds, alter the order of hues
appearing, bring in violins,
cymbals, compose a crescendo
as the sun slipped out of view
into the black hat of night,
waiting for a gloved hand to
pull it out once again over
the slums of Mumbai.

*The Birds are Singing Again*

## Quiet Quiet Now

The dog is curled, sleeping.
Do not startle her. Stay
where you are
for one breath, two,
as many as you need
to see the new day
arrive, hear — the calling
birds, who never forget
to sing.

# I Am Small

Give me back my father kneeling,
nailing planks of sweet cedar on the walls
of the front hall closet. I am small

three maybe four, standing near. I say
"Love me, Daddy." He turns, lays down his hammer
shines that smile as he wraps his two maple tree arms

around me. Give me back my father. Not the one
who threw Mother's Sunday dinner, china plate
against the wall, mashed potatoes glazed with gravy

oozing down in rivulets — the silence after. No
give me back the father who always turned
toward me those nights I crept to his side

of the bed when that misty Ghost of Christmas Past,
chains rattling, arms reaching for me, walked out
of my open, lighted closet — again.

Give me back the joker father at the church picnic
who ran that race, the one where you inhaled
to hold a bean at the end of a straw

then ran as far as you could before the bean fell off.
Give me back the father who ran and ran, past everyone
past me jumping up and down, proud. Proud even

when he refused the prize, laughing, saying he'd lost
the bean after his first four strides. Give me back
his fedora hat, his squared leather briefcase filled

with legalese, give me his bust of Lincoln too —
the one he kept on his office credenza, the one we saw
over his shoulder when he was sitting firm in the swivel chair

of every office he ever had, even the last windowless
one in his basement filled with files and photo albums
that remembered when he no longer could. Give me back

my father, still smiling wide, cracking the double joints
in his thumbs. Showing me — I could too.

# The Birds Are Singing Again

How do they know
morning is coming?
That the sun will rise
again. Know to
trust that first bird who
heralds with unwavering joy —

          Come! Greet morning!
It is still
very dark.

Yet — they are always right.
Night lightens, lessens, moves.

My father told me,
gazing out the window at the
ocean, "I want to come back as a
great gray pelican." Now

when I see pelicans
I see him
showing off his sure glide, those
wide-spanned wings tipping to wave
as he flies on. Or sitting atop a
weathered piling, like a judge
waiting for me to approach
the bench, ask
for a private word.

When they are gone, when they have
fallen out of your world, you look for them —
everywhere.

I wanted to come back
as a humming bird.
All shimmery iridescence,
able to appear still when I am not.
Small and delicate yet able to fly
without stopping from the tip of
the Yucatan to New Orleans, across
the wide glinting Gulf of Mexico. Never
giving up.

But this morning, I say no —
let me be a song bird.
I want to feel the light coming —

          And tell someone.

## Dessert Always Tastes Better When You Eat It First

My grandfather whistled songs
while we walked along the path
through the orchard he'd planted
on land bought and paid for
during the Great Depression because
he never lost his job.

Produce buyer for A&P he met the trains
bringing goods from west to east, eyeing
crates of berries and lettuce, thumping
watermelons, listening for that deep hollow echo —
everyone needed food.

In straight lines, row after row he planted
fruit trees on the land that backed up
to the farm where he's been a boy. Watered,
tended those trees until they held apples and pears,
peaches, plums. Until he could quit his job
at A&P, taking with him all he knew
about the taste of fruits.

He built a solid red brick house
that still stands after seventy years. The house
where my mother, just sixteen moved into
a room of her own. The house where my
father paced the floor on the night I was born.
The house we were walking toward
on the path through the orchard, grandfather
whistling song after song — because

he was afraid to talk. Afraid the stutter
would rise again. The way it did
when he was a boy, the way it could
even now.

I didn't know that, as a child when I walked through
the orchard with him. Didn't know the story my mother
told me years later. How Grandfather's boss
invited him to dinner. How he'd nodded
yes. But when it came time to walk out the door,
he couldn't. Wouldn't leave his chair. How
Grandmother dialed the number
and lied.

All I knew then was that once
when I rode with him in the truck
to the cider mill I heard him tell the men
which apples to use for hard cider
and which ones for sweet juice. And
whenever we walked through that back kitchen door
the first thing he'd do was open the refrigerator
ask how many wanted a glass of cold apple juice.

All I knew was that he never missed
the evening news or the Ed Sullivan Show,
shared Planter's Peanuts with me from the
blue can while we watched. That his favorite
chair was an Easy Boy recliner, and each
evening he took a key, wound the clock
that hung on the living room wall.
Its steady tick tock never faltered.

And I remember when he and grandmother
tucked me in for the night he would always say
as he turned out the light, "See you in the funny papers."

Remember too, how he told us
"Dessert tastes better if you eat it first."
I saw him do it too — only once. Saw Grandmother set down
a plate of apple pie à la mode and watched him eat it all before he reached
for her chicken and dumplings and the good green beans
from their garden. And — how they laughed.

*– in memory of Lewis Solomon*

# Morning Prayer

It's the one that begins
*Dear God* then turns,
churns into *Why?*
*Why him? Why her?*
*Why us?*   Wanders off
beyond her window to the
the stark white snow, the ice
the cold black trees. Returns —
still clinging to the back of
*Why?*   Hesitates
veers to that story of the rabbi
who slaps the seeker's face
because his yearning
was for answers. Crawls then,
the prayer does, into her fingers.
Reaches out to touch his face,
to touch the man still sleeping beside her
after all these years. Then leans
to stroke the dog, curled
warm. Brings her down,
the prayer does
to here, to now, to this.

## They Walk the Same Way

I saw him from a window, books
under his arm, making his way to the library.

I remember smiling when I saw the way he leaned
into the fall wind, the day, what lay ahead. I see him

again as I look, years later, at the picture of our son
walking a familiar beach, walking the same way

his father walks, even now. He too leaning
into the wind, the day, leaning toward

what he dreams lies ahead. Following him —
his own small son, the angle of his short stride

mirroring his father's, both of them bent head first
into the chill, hands tucked into their pockets.

No way to know, for any of us, what waits
unforeseen along the way.

I look again at the picture I hold in my hand.
See now what was always there framed,

crouching in the corner. A cluster
of bittersweet.

*– For Bob and Dominique*

# Write a Poem

about the bougainvillea he says, so we will remember
their bright fuchsia blossoms shining through

our bedroom window, more lush and full than we
have ever seen them. About how two strong stems

are reaching, leaning toward the window as if inviting us to
look again — linger, write about the way, after we draw the sheer

cream drapes across the open window, they sway and lift
the way we do when we are making love. And say it

that way — *making love*
say it that beautiful way

*– Gracias Roberto*

## It Could Have Been Otherwise

Warning. I might grow maudlin, saccharine,
marking another birthday, remembering the Beatles singing
so easily — *When I get older, losing my hair, many years from now.*

Skinny pants, Nehru collars and those bowl cut mops of hair
wondering — *Will you still love me, will you still feed me
when I'm sixty-four.* What did they know then? What

do I know now, about stepping into that once
far away year? And why wince? It could have been
otherwise. My grandmother was gone

at fifty-seven. Mind gone long before that
a cousin told me, remembering the day
she knocked on Grandmother's door, came into

the kitchen. How Grandmother turned to look
at her, staring blankly, the clock ticking
ticking. And then, without saying a word, turned slowly,

too slowly, back to the feel of water, vegetables, only her hands
remembering. It could have been like John Lennon, forty
when he turned, saw the gun, the hand

then nothing more. Those silly innocent lyrics he sang imagining
*Grandchildren on your knee.* Yesterday my grandson
turned nine. His birthday one day before his father's,

two days before mine. On his birthday we went to lunch
with his brother. I brought gifts. The ones he'd hoped for —
Dash the stuffed horse and books that he can read

all by himself. On my birthday I look out my window
at still blue waters, see a lone fishing boat, waiting for perch
to swim by. See the gulls gliding back and forth, swooping

swerving as though choreographed. I wonder about time, how it is
and isn't. How I can still be fifteen even now, the small, gray
box like radio on the desk in my room bringing me

those young, light-hearted lyrics — still sending me
*a valentine, birthday greeting, bottle of wine*

# In the Cemetery

The green metal basket my mother and I place
on my father's grave, is live with color —
red geraniums, yellow marigolds,
the purple and white of alyssum.

Nearby, an old man, his farmer's jeans and work shirt
well faded, suspenders taut across the swell of his belly,
scatters seed "to green the family graves," he tells us —
his two brothers, a sister, his mother, his father.

Seeing the grave we tend, he says, to my mother,
"Knew your husband's people well. Bought horses
at the auction from his Pa, Andy. They lost the one boy,
young, didn't they?" He nods toward a nearby stone.
The boy's name, etched between the mother's,
the father's.

"You know," the old man says, "you got those flowers
on the wrong side of the stone. Front side's just for show.
For people drivin' by. Body's on the other side." He points.
"He's lying here."

The night my father died, I dreamed he was on a train. I was on it too.
Unsteady, unsure, he had hesitated when the train stopped, when
the doors first opened. The train, starting again, slowed for a curve
and the doors, which should not have opened then, did.
The train still moving — he jumped, landing lightly.
He did not look back.

The old farmer, my mother and I —

There are no bodies here.
We tend places where they were.

# Ode to Change

See —
the early
morning sky
is black
again.
Stars, moon
linger longer.
The winds,
coming
from the north
more often
now have
pitch, whine
thin and
high.
Waves turn up
their volume,
roar to shore
slapping sand
into curves,
carve inlets, lift
sandbars.
Poplars, Oaks
Cottonwoods, Sumac
climb the slant
of rising dunes
turning again —
red, rust, lucent
orange, yellow.
And there is
nothing you
can do
to stop the world
turning, moving
farther from the sun.
Nothing you
need to do.
Only remember
Only breathe

## Fly Boy, Fly

In grainy black and white, you pose
on the wing of a plane. A flyboy.

They told you the lessons were free and you
saw an easy sling shot ride

out of that four corner town, thought
high in the sky it would all fall away —

the father who played but never won, the mother
who grieved the other son. "Free,"

they said. And you, standing there on the wing
of a plane, don't know the hell you'll pay,

don't know about the Water Beast, its carrier deck long as the main
street in your small town, how you will dispatch planes — cry out,

"More loft! More loft!" — then lurch, watch, as the Beast's prow plows under
one more innocent flyboy. You don't know how torpedoes will aim where you sleep,

don't yet know the scream, "Kamikazes! 12 o'clock! 3 o'clock!" or how they
fall, flame. Don't know the stench of charred mates. That's why you still smile

standing there, preserved in black and white, you don't know —
You will live. Live to father four. Never care for boats. Keep flying.

When you grow too old to fly, you will still climb up, onto that wing,
settle in the cockpit, drive in and out of your hollow, hallowed hangar.

In the next life, you promised — you'd come back as a bird.
Do that.

*– for Lieutenant Russell H. Volkema*

## Keep Going This Way

Come down to the water's edge on a clear sky
summer morning when the only sounds
are the waves shuffling back and forth
and a few sparkling gulls calling

as they glide above the Great Lake. Come
plant your feet in the cool sand, let the waves
lap your feet like a dog's soft velvety tongue. Feel
the water invite you in. Go slowly. One step,

another — the water eddies around your ankles. Keep going
the water laps your knees, thighs. Cool water turning colder,
deepening to your waist. Keep going this way
if you can. Or plunge. Commit all at once, the way

the little boy did, the one you watched from shore last night,
shouting to his brother to watch him dive all the way in,
then sprang back up, looking fast over his shoulder
to see if his brother was still watching,

his head back, laughing, ready
to do it again, now he knew
he could.

# When You Feel That Old Fear Coming Towards You, Here's What You Do

Pick up a book, any book, read words, get lost
    in a story, a poem, the Sunday comics, two recipes from
    *Think Food: Brain Healthy Recipes.*

Give yourself an A for effort. I mean you take Fish Oil, DHA, Curcumin
    and every other supplement anyone mentions
    that might possibly prevent plaques in the brain.

Do another Lumosity brain game on your computer,
    though you read that all you're really doing
    is getting better and better at computer games.

Recite the names of your elementary school teachers —
    Mrs. Ridenhour, Mrs. Lily, Mr. Tuhvel, Mr. Crook (really his name.)

Forgive yourself when you can't remember the name
    of your kindergarten teacher, the one with the beautiful black hair
    who turned down the lights and taught you about "rest time." Or the name
    of your first grade teacher, the one who showed you that letters
    make words and words made Dick and Jane run.

Think of something positive —
    like tonight he'll notice the kitchen trash is overflowing,
    the college kids won't crank up their music, and you'll have
    all the right ingredients for that brain healthy recipe.

Don't think about how your brilliant father, at seventy-five
    forgot the entry code to his garage,
    and later — forgot his way home.

Breathe in    Breathe out
    the way they do on the meditation tape
    the one you listen to each morning.

Look out your window
    see the sailboats skittering north,
    listen to the birds, welcoming morning, smile because summer
    is green and flowering — even if
    the name of that tree and those pink flowers, the ones you've always loved,
    has gone the way of other names that start with "p."

Take a walk with the dog through the woods or down the beach,
    fill the bird feeder, check to see which blossoms bloomed overnight
    all probably better for you than doing one more Lumosity game.

Revise this poem.

And whenever that old fear of Alzheimer's draws near, whispering —
    Your grandmother's name. Your father's name. Your aunt's name.
    Your cousin's name — the one who died this morning,
    the one not much older than you.

Stick out your tongue. Shake your fist.
And remember — the night he asked you to dance.

## Prayer of the Cockroach

Oh God,
I know —
    I trespass.

I scuttle beneath
the skirts of their
proper beds, taint
their clean
counters, dart
from crannies,
frightening the
upright.

Forgive me
if still, I ask —

Protect me
from the limelight,
the glare that draws
eye and mind
to this sleek, black
body, as I make
my outrageous climb
up white washed
walls.

Save me
from those who
shudder
who fear my fervor
to replenish the earth
with multitudes more
like myself who know
how to outrun

the heel of the boot
the slap, squash
of the swat,
that ends.

O God,
in the very shadow
of those who would
lord over me
        — make me fast

## Walking the Beach

I see
       what you no longer can.

How the dogs still rush
to scatter the gathered gulls —

who lift, fly of course
bright confetti, flickering
white
       against pure blue

  *Are you near?*

Look. You can see
where they have been
the lacey pattern
of their webbed feet
are everywhere.

I want to set a chair
for each of you who are
gone now
along the water's
edge —
       *There are more of you*
       *every year now, more.*

I will make one long front row
so you can see autumn come again,
see the trees that climb the dunes
going gold, red, russet.

The poplars still
hold out. They
cling to lemon-lime.

And look —
the beach grasses are
sprouting seed heads

 *I want you*
       *to stay.*

## My Choice

to let yellow days
leave
without wandering
through trees
and trillium
and the old trails
of Indians.

The watch
I wear on my wrist
swears —
no time
to stand
still

after hearing
twigs breaking
bodies rustling
through brush

sign
that deer
are near.

Every time.
My choice.

Whether
to turn.

# Valentine

> *Just this little time and*
> *perhaps a little more*
> — Jack Ridl, *Suite for the Turning of the Year*

Tell me again
how little time. No
show me. Show me

the puffed throat of
the Cactus Wren
just before he begins

to trill. Show me the sun
sneaking into the sky
just before the colors

startle into day.
Dare me
to stand still

breathing
counting
not just to ten.

Feeling now
the slight breeze
skimming

across my skin
lifting leaves, petals
wisps of your hair.

Then, in this little time
hearing you whisper
*Love me.*

*– for Bob*

# When You Have Nothing to Say

Sit still

Sit still even longer

*Through the Fog*

## The Trajectory

I didn't expect a straight shot
angled skyward, or even a smooth
horizontal line heading unimpeded
west or east. But

    and there it is, the word

that stops all forward motion.
    The word that hesitates,
    looks around, shakes
    a head, even cries
        sometimes.

        But then

                moves on.

# Tell Me

how, above us
birds balance
on high wires
side by side like
letters, inked on
a ruled line. I try
to decipher words,
try to hear messages
in their ragged songs.
Above them, gnarled fists
of winter clouds deny
the sun. How do
they keep from flailing
forward, spinning back?
How does she? Missing
the child — in that chair,
in his bed, in the air.
How does the soldier
still stride, bearing
blood, bodies, his
legs — bursting in air?
How do they hear the
doctor's words, defy
gravity, stand up, walk
through the door, as the
doctor looks down then
left, out the window.

Tell me how
clenching the wire —
they sing?

# This Time

it wasn't funny, hearing the famous poet
read his poem. The one about forgetting,
how the title is the first to go, followed by

the author's name, the plot. How books you kept
close, spines erect on bookshelves, old friends —
become only vaguely familiar

strangers. Not funny now, since you
have been with her. How for awhile,
you couldn't tell. Same smile,

same low laugh, still able to appreciate
a good oxymoron. Her questions, not
at all strange, the first time, or even

the second time. All of us forget now
and then whether we've said aloud what we
were wondering. It was when she asked,

still curious, with the same words, the same
lilt, the same question again, and then again
and then again. Each time

you nodded, smiled, answered as if
for the first time. As if you didn't notice
how she was sliding from view, like

the sailboat you saw yesterday, out your
window — headsail, mainsail aloft, sailing
left to right, the way we read. Looming

large, stolid as it sailed close to shore, yet inch
by inch disappearing — prow first, then headsail, mast
devoured by the hard edge of the window's frame.


    *– for Mickie*

## News, Sports and Weather

You think maybe today will be different.
You think this time the beautiful blond
newscaster who recently replaced
the slightly overweight brunette, the one
who reminded you of your mother, will
have some good news — Say one
of the wars has ended, or that Republicans
and Democrats are once again sharing
the same cafeteria, balancing service trays
side by side, both reaching for
meatloaf and mashed potatoes. But no —

the Barbie doll blond prefers
to polish death to a fine gleam, show us
again that clip of amateur film, body parts
and blood blown sky high at a finish line. Then,
bowing her head she announces tearfully
that another six year old shot his two year old
sister, by accident. It was no accident.
The gun was where it always was, in the drawer
of the side table, on his father's side
of the bed. There to protect
the family.    You had hoped, when you pressed

the power button on your universal remote
that today she might mention the mockingbird
she saw perched pertly on the tip of a magnolia branch,
might point out the repertoire of songs this small bird mimics
to announce a new day with a second chance to smile
at a neighbor, offer that cup of cold water. Or maybe
report the rescue of those ducklings, the ones that had fallen
one by one into the storm drain.  But no — she wants
to interrupt us with breaking news that the woman
we've seen on the screen every day for four months,
the one who sliced and stabbed and repeatedly

shot her former boyfriend has been found guilty,
is on suicide watch. Then, smoothly she segues
back to the hammer of her litany informing us the
death toll in that collapse of another shoddy factory,
over there where they make clothes we wear, has risen
to over a thousand. Even the one sop of good news —
three women, after ten grisly years, have escaped
their abductor — comes swaddled in such a dark cloak
of depravity that you find it hard to breathe,
believe.   Once upon a time someone asked,

"Why not News, Poetry, Sports and Weather." And don't you
wonder — if we'd dare to make that leap — whether even one
small poem each day would anchor us, hold our feet to
miracles passing. Like the way that outrageously long stem
of fuchsia bougainvillea looks like a child reaching
for more. Or how last night when you rolled over, half asleep,
pulled the covers up over your shoulders, he was still
there, still breathing. Maybe, then, the slightly
overweight brunette would still have a job.

# Through the Fog

Morning comes
scarcely
it's thin, emaciated

light offering
only bare outlines
of the landmarks I know

are there —
slender poplars,
dune grass greening

the water I hear
lapping softly
along the shore.

The day's prediction
is for storms, change
that cannot be

stopped. Or
changed.
Explains

why
I feel like
rain.

# I Didn't Know

what you needed. I
was watching
finding my way —

in the way I always
do when I find myself
hesitant in the unfamiliar.

And you were new
among us. Bright eyes,
wide smile, inviting.

Was it your way
to protect what
can hurt, what still

hurts? What I want
to say is that I felt
lost

the way I do
in a house of mirrors
running into walls I thought

were windows. What I want
to say is, I never meant
to harm. What I want to say is

take my hand. Here —
we can.

# Did She Carry Him Because He Was Old?

She carried her dog as she walked,
like a mother carrying her child,
his head, resting on her shoulder, looking back
even as the two of them moved forward,
her one free hand stroking his sandy curls.

Perhaps she had carried him this way
since he was a puppy. Full grown, he was not
a large dog, but still —
        heavy for a young girl to carry.

Perhaps it was like that man who
each day carried his calf from the barn
to graze in the field. Every morning, the calf
a little heavier — but just a little — so that
it was never too much, what he had to bear.
And so for him it was not so great a feat
after all those years, to carry a full grown cow
from the barn to the field to graze.

Or maybe the dog had stepped on a sharpness,
as they were walking, in the normal way, side by side.
Yowled pain, lifted a paw to show her
he couldn't walk, not all the way home.
It might have been that. There was a leash still attached
to his collar, and she held the end in one hand.

Or maybe this was a last walk. The dog, looking back,
already running ahead. And she, holding on.

# Now and Then

*– for my father*

I see him, seeing it again, his eyes
staring. How he bows his head,

then weeps into his bowl of soup.
"Don't know what's wrong with me."

Meaning his tears. Meaning
more than his tears.

His spoon suspended half-way,
soup slipping back into the bowl

he shakes his grayed head.
Disbelieving what happened then.

What is happening now.
"It was Fall, 1944, San Diego Bay.

They told me to pack my bags, time
to leave that posh hotel the Navy

commandeered. Six sailors to a room.
I'd worked my way up to a bed —

but orders, time to ship out.
No more stepped on board then

the plane tried to land on the carrier
deck. Stalled. Missed the catch cable."

I see his eyes go soft, wet, then distant
again "Arms," he says, "Arms, legs

flying everywhere. And blood.
All that blood."

They sent him back,
back to the Hotel Coranado.

New sailor in the bed he thought
he'd never need again. Rages then,

calls the M.P.'s. "They gave me back
the bed." He looks down, lifts

the spoon to his mouth again. No longer
who he was. Decapitated now.

Lost at sea. Why can't we
call the M.P.'s? Tell them, tell them

to give him back his mind

# What If God is Praying to Us?

Why not? Created in the image,
as we purportedly are don't you
think the Great Divine, that Three
in One or whatever you name it,
might expect each and every one of us
to do our part? I can't imagine
God intended our sole contribution
would be naming the animals! I mean
given how we've been endowed don't you
think God envisioned us putting our
shoulders to the wheel, shoulder
to shoulder? Tending the garden, spreading
the news that heaven doesn't need
to wait, can happen here, can happen
now, even — among us. Remember
the deal? "I shall bless you so that
you shall be a blessing." Suggests,
don't you think, some human
initiative? I mean, what if right now
She's looking down the barrel of the future,
strumming the table, seeing there may not
be another millennium in the cards. Maybe
not even another decade at the rate we're brandishing
Free Will — that weapon of Mass Destruction.
What if, she's watching us, peering at us through that
Thin Place, as the Celts called it, praying without
ceasing that we grow up, put away
childish things, stop this eye for an eye that
leaves everybody blind. Praying we stop
this riotous cheering every time the other side
takes a lethal hit. (Not everything is a sporting event!)
If we listen up, maybe we'd hear God chanting
without ceasing, "Turn your swords into ploughshares."
Or is the chant changing? "Turn your swords and your *words*
turn them into ploughshares." I'm asking —
What if God is praying to us because
we are God's heart and hands, mind and eyes in this
break-your-heart-beautiful world. And how long —
will God keep praying? Until there is nothing?
Except the insects and the grasses
and the stars?

# Poem I Don't Want Read
# On My 80th Birthday

Why didn't you stop, wherever you were, stop walking, stop talking, stop doing whatever it was you were doing? Why didn't you stop, stock still, ten, or even twenty times a day? Why did you keep racing past all those years, leaning forward?

Why didn't you stop, twirl, see those tomatoes still ripening on the counter, reach down to touch the dog you knew was dying curled at your feet, look instead of gliding by those pictures framed and arranged on your bookshelves with books you were sure you would read again, the boy still five, the girl unfolding into woman, the man's hair still dark, his skin smooth, yours too?

Why didn't you pay homage each morning to the sky brightening, the clouds drifting, the water stretching to the horizon, beach grass bending, that white sail leaning into the wind?

Why didn't you make a sacrament of holding your breath? Remember, when you were a child, how you held your breath, swimming underwater the whole length of the pool? When you pulled yourself up out of the deep end, your chest heaving, gasping for air, you knew what you took for granted.   Why —

decade after decade when you woke in the middle of the night, saw the moon through the window shimmering light across the water, why did you turn away, worry if you remembered to add blueberries to the grocery list, pull the covers closer — and sleep?

# Gone the Sun

### I.

In Mexico, we see the police car, lights flashing, approach
moving slowly, no siren — no urgency.

We turn the corner, see the dark hearse, the old,
the young, heads bowed following — spilling across

the narrow street. Interspersed among them, bright red
pick-ups, their truck beds laden with flowers.

Last — the lone rider on his black motorcycle
wearing a skeleton mask.

### II.

In India the woman at Ghandi's grave lays a hand
over her heart, "I will care for you."

Touches fingers to her lips,
"I will speak of you."

Kisses the tips of her fingers, touches them
To her brow, "I will think of you."

### III.

Outside the funeral home, the slow
haunting notes of Taps.
Day is done

# There is Nothing You Can Do

for the boy, the small boy on his way, on his way from here to there across the way, across the road, the little boy who does not see the cars, the cars, that have no eyes that have no ears that cannot see, that cannot hear his foot fall, the little foot, the one he lifts the one that steps into the way from here to there, the cars, the cars that do not see that do not hear his other foot the one that follows right behind, the way it would the way it does if you must run from here to there across the way, across the road and do not know that there is nothing cars can do, the cars, the cars that come and go, how could he know, the small boy, who feels so fast remembers now how fast he was the day he ran, round and round the table ran, to show them all how fast he goes, so strong, so fast, he knows the way, he has no time, no time to wonder why we all must die and there is nothing you can do.

## This One is for You

All around us two is breaking
into one. His heart stops
while she is still getting ready
to go out without him. She wonders
why he doesn't answer when she calls
good-bye. Now, every day she goes out
without him, comes home —
one again.

Another woman reads, then signs
the stiff white pages, legalese
severing what was once, what
might have been. Two
untangling into ones. Still
there are children knotted between
who will not come undone. Children —
the river between their opposing banks.

Two other lovers tremble,
feel the earth moving under
their feet, startled to see
fissures opening —
the gap growing between
the sharp, raw edges of
their differences. Teetering
at the edge of an endless falling
falling away from what they dreamed
would be. Longing not
to let go.

We two, older now
grow closer
to what was always
true — a day when only one
of us will wake, see
another sun. This soft spring
morning, as you lie sleeping
next to me, hear me whisper
*I'm glad we are still two.*
Feel my hand reaching,
intertwining still
with yours.

# Counting

She hears thunder. Then sees
the flash of lightning slash across
the early morning sky. A change

from days of cloudless blue, a sun that burns
the crops this overheated summer. She
stays inside, culling books from

bookshelves. Unread books
she knows now she will never
read. No longer cares to read.

Now and then, as she stacks the books
on piles near the door, a title nags, begs
reprieve. She flicks through pages

sees the kind of words that once held her.
But she is not who she was then. It's time
to let them go. Lightning again.

She glances up, looks out her window
at a clarity of light. Remembers
when she was a child, how she learned

to count the seconds between each flash of lightning
and the rumble of thunder. Counting so she knew
how close the storm. And when — finally

it was moving away.

# Don't Just Stand There — Scream! Run!

That's what I want to say every time I see you
in that black and white photo, the one with
    *Ma and Pa — 1943*
written below, in my father's hand.

I want you to blink, want you to come
back from wherever you are,
gazing up and left, looking demented.
Which, in 1943, you probably already are.

I want your blood
to warm again. Want to see
your hands wrench free
from that proper clasp, see them flutter, flap

then slap the smile off that little man
standing next to you, his cheap woolen scarf
wound round his neck like an ascot. The one
who showed up only for pictures, all jokes and jive.

I want to see your flat-lined lips crack wide open.
Want you to howl as you loosen the pins from
the knot at the nape of your neck, the knot
that holds back the hair,
                      too white too soon.

Let your mane flare wild as you shrug off that stone
gray coat with its too faux fur collar.
Show us *you*, naked beneath, not a stitch left of what
might have been. Which is why, even now,

I want you to step out of that black and white
box photo and into this picture. The one I hold
in my other hand.
        You, seventeen

leaning back,
against your mother's long skirted knees.
Your eyes, daring anyone
                to stop you


*– for Hazel Reminga Volkema (1895-1952)*

# On Seeing Again — My Father's Face

I should have known you'd find a way
to be here — though you can no longer
take my hand in yours. My hand

so like your hand. Same square shape,
though not as large. Mine a woman's hand. Still
I can span an octave and a half. When

I plinked out the melody of *Für Elise* with one
hand, the way my friend taught me, you were sure
I was a prodigy, bartered lessons

for me, believed that cultured, I'd never
slip back down that rabbit hole where fathers
failed and failed and mothers wished

you had never been born. You would never let us
wonder if we were loved, so I should have
known you would come, appear

in the framed photograph that fell five shelves,
landing without shattering. Lifted up
from the floor, there you were, smiling

the way you always smiled, even in the dark
when I tugged on your sleeve waking you,
whispering —

whispering even now, *I am afraid.*

# Put Down Your Pack

You can now.
It's over.
All of it — over. Let

the straps that hung
heavy, that cut into
your shoulders

slip off, first one
then the other. Let go
the fetid memory

of what you can never
change. Put down
your pack. Leave it

on the steep trail
you were forced
to walk.

So much at stake —
if you lost your footing
the edge gave way.

Leave the stones
you carried. Leave
them

in the pack. Do not
use them to build
an altar. Keep

walking. See
the white butterflies
dancing flower to flower.

See the Lake glinting,
the even line of the horizon,
the terrain leveling out before you.

Be you again. You won't know
what still could come
to meet you. Or

how you will keep going
when it does. But you will.
You know that now.

Take this.
Take only this
with you.

    *– for my brother Daniel*

# Say It Plain

In the early morning dark, she knew.
Which is why she did not hurry to answer
the phone, or to move out from under the covers,
out into the day where he was not.

Say it plain. She was glad — *glad*
that he had not died on her watch.
She did not believe, as her brother did,
that if you were there at the tick of time
when the dying departed, you might be able to tell
if there was something more than this one life.

Though at times she hoped it might be true,
she didn't believe enough to risk being there,
risk that her last memory of him would be cast —
mouth gone slack, eyes emptied, and the head,
the once proud head, nothing now
but hard bone and slipping flesh.

A week ago, she sat on the edge of his bed
and whispered, "If you want to go,
don't eat, don't drink."

Now, after answering the phone, hearing the words
she knew she would hear, she is still listening
to the clock tick, wishing there had been more time.

Breathing him out.   Breathing him in

# The Sea

Death's whispering.
Another wave. And
another after that.

## Let the Poem Come to You

It was there, right in front of me
the setting moon I mean, coming to me
full orb hanging low, large, gold
above the water. Fishing boats cut across
its path of yellow light. Trailing behind quietly
a sailboat approaches the same path, its sail
a shadow, small light aloft the mast. I want to say
this time I did not turn away, move on
to what needed doing. I want to say
I stayed. Saw the moon slide free of clouds
angled slant like a beret across its brow.
Saw the same moon grow larger,
slipping into the horizon. I know
they say the moon is the same whether low
in the sky, or high. Know it is our lingering need
to be clear — what is near, far. What is
friend. What is not. To be certain that what we
see is only the moon, changing from gold
to pink. Now — turning pale, ceding rank to the
rising sun, dissolving into dawn.
Like this poem. But the moon. Still the moon.

*In My Time Capsule*

# Little Man

Yesterday, we watched baby turtles making their way
to the sea. Hundreds, newly hatched, gathered from nests

scattered along the shore by those who protect them, released
at sunset. *Be careful, don't try to help too much.*

Warning us — little ones need all the time it takes
to reach the water's edge. Need time to strengthen

legs, feel the shift of sand, learn how footprints are valleys, learn
how to scrabble up and out again. They need to learn how the sea

draws them in, then casts them out on their backs. Need to learn
how to right themselves — again. It wasn't easy, Little Man

to hold ourselves back, resist helping one crawling, falling
behind. Hard to watch as others climbed up and over in their

rush to the sea. We see things they don't — Cormorants, Gulls,
Pelicans eyeing their small heads on land and then at sea

where they lift them above the waterline to breathe. We know
crabs have teeth that crush soft shells, innocent bodies. *Few will survive.*

We nod, know that even for those who do, there will be change they
will not want — and suffering. We nod, but then reach for one left, lost

in a hollow valley, remembering we became human caring for kin, learning
the language of neighbor, friend. Once, then twice we lift, carry, clear

a path. Little Man — swim. So many dreams you carry across the seas
on your soft, small shell.


*– for Jacob Robert DeNooyer*

# Remembering Seagulls

Today, as I walked the beach I watched
a flock of seagulls lift up
as I neared, spread their wings
scatter towards the blue summer sky —
then drift out over the great Lake,
their white bodies glittering
with morning sun.

I saw us again sitting at the edge
of the dunes, summer, drawing maps
to show where gulls gathered each day.
Their numbers increasing, peaking,
then declining as September drew near.

Remembered again that morning
after you had gone. The beach
September quiet. No bright colored
umbrellas opened against the sun. No children
jumping waves, shouting to parents —
wanting them to see how brave they are.
Only a flock of gulls, gathered
then rising, moving on.

There had been tears the morning
you left. Not just mine.
Your tears slipping into Frosted Flakes,
as you sat at the counter. And tears,
as you posed next to your father on the deck,
your car packed, ready, with all you thought
you would need.

Then, and even now, the house misses your
eager voice. I smile — glad for seagulls. Say to you,
say to myself — Keep flying,
keep rising, keep going.


*- for Dominique*

# Bread and Wine

So often the smell of fresh bread
as I walked through the door,
home after school. And you

in the kitchen, your apron
dusty with flour, the apron
you wore to save your everyday

flower patterned housedress,
the kind everyone's
mother wore. I see

the loaves, their butter
slicked crusts, cooling on
the wire racks, bread you make

because it pleases him. Your
life orbits what pleases — him
us, our needs, our wants.

Except for that hour
late afternoon, just before dinner.
I'd find you sitting on the sofa

in the living room reading
the afternoon paper,
elegantly holding half

a glass of dark red wine.,
sipping it leisurely as you turned
the pages. Today — the day after

my brother calls to tell me
you are gone — I can smell
the scent of fresh baked bread,

wish I could see you
savor one more sip of wine.


– *for my mother, Lois Jean Solomon*

# After Words

*– for Daphne (2000-2013) and all my beloved Bichons*

I.

When I stroke
your small head, you
open clouded eyes
see shadows, see
me, then drift again
into sleep.

II.

I carry you,
walk the road
you used to walk
with me, through
woods, trails
wanting for you
and me a eulogy
in memories — you
no leash, running
nosing leaves and logs,
following the traces
of anonymous scents.

III.

We have done this before,
beneath this same tree circled
with other stones, marked
with other names. He
leans into the shovel,
the earth. I watch.
Each time I wonder —
why. Why they
must leave. See
the small grave,
opened now
waiting.

IV.

I choose a shroud,
the plaid wool blanket once
my Irish grandfather's, then
my mothers, then mine. Like this
small Bichon — bequeathed.
Mother, our Daphne stayed
two years. I tell you
so you will know
to welcome her.

V.

I see the black
wrought iron chair
still slightly pulled away
from the table, angled
so I could watch
the sun setting, see
the clouds turn
once more to gold
then pink, the sky shade
to purple blue
while I held you,
while the good
doctor who came
to spare you fear,
probed for a vein,
that would open
a door.

VI.

Creator of all that lives
and breathes, who mingles
among us through
the ones we love —
Receive now
the gentle spirit of
this small beloved,
so faithful to all
who touched her life.
Enfold her in your
good earth. Keep her
safe, until at last
she is one again
with the trees, the leaves
the trail.

# Morning Sky

Yesterday, I found your crayon,

and I miss you. Miss your four-year-old eyes, the way
every day they see something new. Remember
that morning early, you and your brother, older

by two years, nested in bed, whispering, pointing
out the window as I enter. Seeing me you say —

> *Oh, you almost missed it Grandma!*

I look, see — layer on layer of neon
above the calm sea. It was no sky
you and I had ever seen before. Blue scrim

brightened into turquoise, stripes of yellow
darkening to gold, pink burning the underbelly
of purple. And more — bright orange rimmed

with smears of cloud. Your brother ran to find
clean paper and your little bags of colors, the ones
you always bring along with you. I look

out the window, see the colors already fading. Yesterday
I learned my cousin is beginning to forget.
She is ten years older than I am. Almost the age

her mother was when she began forgetting. Like my father,
like my grandmother. I don't want to forget

your blond head bent over paper. Your small
fingers working the crayons, laying down colors on
the clean, white page. How you began

with an arc of turquoise, added pink,
purple, and then another blue,
Mexican Blue you said.

> *Hurry I need that yellow —*

Your brother nods, hands it to you, understands.
There is so little time to catch the sky.


– *for Wyatt*

# Life After Forty

That year I turned forty you turned sixteen, beginning
to show the curves of a womanly body, turning heads
whenever you walked by. You still do —

even after this blur of years has raced past both of us.
Now you are stepping into forty.

When I turned forty they told me I'd reached life's peak,
reminded me to look back down the mountain, see
how far I'd come, what I'd done and didn't do. Paths

I didn't take — and why. I'd see wrong turns, dead ends and the path
that led me to the peak. Turning, I'd start down the mountain's
other side heading home, all I'd learned would guide me.

I know better now at sixty-four.

There is no traveling down the mountain, the summit
is still ahead, the incline steeper not gentler.
The mountain greater than I imagined.

I may not still be near when you arrive at sixty-four,
so let me tell you now — a walking stick or someone close
to lean on can help keep your balance. You need to stop,

rest more often, the last leg to the summit will be rigorous.
You'll find too, glancing back what once loomed large
feels smaller, less important now. On some days

clouds still gather. But you'll break through — see clear
blue again, feel the warm sun easing old aches.
Pay attention to eagles as you go. It's not too late

to learn from them — they reach the summit soaring.


– *for Nicole*

# For My Son at Thirty-Two

You were nine, running down the beach
                    ahead of me, on that hot summer night
looking back over your shoulder, ready
                    to receive the football I awkwardly threw.
You lunged, going wide for it,
                    happy to tumble into the cool waters
grinning as you rose, body glistening,
                    the ball held high as the waves
applauded — pass complete.
                    At fourteen, I found you sitting on the edge of your
bed, hesitating to move into the day. It was still dark
                    beyond the windows. Your eyes met mine
as you said, "You know — I might not make the team."
                    I knew not to wrap my arms around you then.
I knew, you might cry. At fourteen
                    you didn't want to cry. You made the team.
Now, thirty-two, married, I must tilt my head back to meet
                    your eyes as you say, "She lost the baby, again."
And I hear what you don't say, "I might not be a father."
                    Again I don't put my arms around you. I know.
Now — she has held your hand to her womb. You have felt
                    your child's wild preparing to be born. You dream
a son. See him running ahead, looking back over his shoulder
                    to receive. It won't matter I tell you, girl or boy — both
can run, lunge into the air, fall into the waves. Either can be held
                    high. To the sun.
                                      You are running, down the beach.

# In Your Time Capsule I Will Put

Your smile.

That Friday lunch at Sandy Point when a friend asked, "Has he found anyone yet?"
Then told me about you.

The email — almost a resumé of you — the one I sent, wondering
if he might want to call you.

How the next day he drove to Chicago with friends, and saw your sister there. Classmates
they were, from high school.

Your sister calling — to give you his resumé.

How Monday you walked into work and your boss, my friend said,
"You might be getting a phone call."

His phone call to you.

The first time we met you — Everyday People's Cafe. You leaning toward him.

Your smile.

The thank you card you sent with the view at Punta Mita,
the one I framed, the one still there on the wall.

You, a bride in white, listening to his promises, then offering yours.

That phone call, four years later — on the way to the hospital.
The picture sent hours later. You're holding Jacob, Dominique's arm around you both.

Jacob, nestled in your lap, helping you turn the pages as you read to him.

Another phone call — not quite two years later. Ethan and Alex arriving.

That black Chevrolet Tahoe with three car seats. The way you blossomed into motherhood.
And the way you look at your three boys.

Your favorite songs — the ones you love to sing with, eyes closing, head tilling back.

Your smile.

Saturdays in the summer — the year there was just enough beach.

A tree sheltered drive leading to the land with a view of the Lake.

The house you will build there.

A horizon without end.

*– for Julie*

## The Dancer

You entered — asking her
                to dance. That wedding, you both
still single. She wasn't as sure

of the beat, how to move
                the way you did, feeling
that rhythm pulsing

in your blood, needing
                to set it free, let it fly
through arms, legs

hips loose and rolling.
                You spun her out and in
the way you spun me round

at your wedding, groom dancing
                with mother of the bride,
taking my hand, leading me

kindly. I've watched you dance
                even in your kitchen. Two stepping
between simmering pots, gliding

effortlessly from stove to oven. I'd heard
                you played tennis once, like a dancer,
body synchronized to approach,

turn, swing. And now, mid-point
                you tune your body and your rhythm
to Iron Man dances, poised

to swim, ride, run. The world
                is not always kind to dancers.
Not feeling what they feel,

not compelled as dancers are
                to step out and in, spin
round, begin again, feeling

their way toward new steps,
                drawing close, letting go


*– for Christopher*

## The Two of You

On a summer day in June, you slipped
from your mother's womb one

after the other as easily as the two
yolks that surprised me one morning

when the two of them emerged
from that one shell, making me smile —

We had learned you would both be boys,
miracle of machines seeing through

the shape of things to come. We watched
your mother's body stretching, rounding

giving you all the room she could for you two
to grow. And then you came — eased

into this world a little early.
Alex first, then Ethan. Not identical.

For always fraternal. One day
if people wonder, *Are they even brothers?*

those deep dimples your mother passed on
will give you away. I'm watching you

take teetering steps into your first full
year of being. Watching you toddle, topple.

Waiting now to feel you reach out to us
with your first few words. Lucky boys

always remembering what it was like, to wake
each morning, knowing the other

was there, to start another new day
with you.


*– for Ethan and Alex*

## "This Snow is Delicious"

You said
As you
shoveled scoops
of first snow
your red shovel
dipping into bright
white, offering
me your way
in a world
that chills, where days
grow shorter, darkness
gathers beyond curtained
windows.

Thank you for singing
along with your
movie friend in your
certain voice

> *You've got a friend in me,*
> *yes, you've got a friend in me.*

And thank you
for the way, when your
foot caught in the spokes
of your brother's stroller
and you didn't know
if you could walk,
you said, as the little
toy soldier did

> *Go on without me. It's ok, just go.*

I will little man —
one day, go on
without you. Want
that. Want the old ones
going before the young.
Enough of wars and
rumors of wars. I want
more lions lying down
with lambs. And want to
believe what you promise

    *It's ok — I will catch up.*


    *– for Jacob, age 3*

## You Did Not Want To Stay

You died the same week as Elizabeth Taylor
whose movies you refused to watch after
she left Eddie Fisher for Richard Burton
when they were filming *Cleopatra*
together. Died of the same disease too —
your heart spilling blood into your
lungs and your liver, your kidneys.
And in those last days, taking even
your appetite. You who could bake
a dozen chocolate chip cookies
and eat half of them before
we came home from school.

I remember when your mother
died. She was ninety-three
living in a nursing home,
dying in a nursing home.
The last time I saw her
I remember she looked down
at her hands resting quietly
on either side of her disappearing
body and asked, bewildered,
*Whose hands are these?*
She died while I was away
on vacation. You said not to worry,
no need to come home for the funeral.

You died too, while I was away.
The last time I saw you alive,
I had to put the pail beneath
that toilet they put by the bed
in your living room, so you wouldn't
soil your pistachio green carpet.
Carpet you got to choose after
he was gone. Not claiming it was
the perfect choice because, you said,
*I gave up perfect after the third child.*

I don't believe that. Or if you
gave it up you never forgot
what perfect looked like. Or that
your body wasn't — though you tried
every diet known to man.
For Christmas one year
he bought you a membership
to the YWCA so you could swim
and exercise and grow thin.

I don't know if you believed there was more
than this one life. But you felt him near
you said. When you brushed your teeth,
you'd look into the mirror half expecting
to see him behind you, watching to see
if you were using warm water the way
he always reminded you was better.

I still hear you singing
that lullaby, the one you sang
to me, the one you sang to
every grandchild —

*O ta loola loola loola loola bye bye.*
*You can have the moon to play with*
*and the stars to run away with,*
*if only you won't cry.*

The one I still sing.

*– for you Mom (1924-2011)*

# On Your Birthday

Okay. I am here, writing — writing
about you. I remembered. Saw it coming

on the calendar. May 23, your birthday.
You would be ninety-four, if you were here

watching the newscasters talk about invading
Normandy Beach seventy years on. And you would tell me again

of your part in that war, though you were on a flight deck on an ocean
halfway round the world. Eighteen months at sea without ever

putting ashore. Which is why, you told me once, you never wanted
to own your own boat.

You left us paragraph by paragraph, sentence
by sentence, word by word. And you saw it coming —

what dismantled your mother, her brother, your sister.
I conjure you up, see you the way you were, dressed

for work. Suit, white shirt, clip-on tie with its perfect knot. I see you
holding up that check — the fee you earned for a case well

won. You wanted to make sure I knew, what I might not
otherwise — you gave of every check you earned, the first fruits

to the Church, to give to those who needed shoes and shelter,
like you needed when you were a child. I still feel your arms

wrapped all the way around my small body,
keeping me safe until I was ready to wander off. I took you

with me. Took your longing to right wrongs. And your
melancholy that one lifetime was not enough.

I miss you. And yet still feel you near. Like today.
When I 'm sure it's you, whispering in my ear, nudging me

to write. Reminding me to bring you back to life.


*– for Russell Harry Volkema (1920-2001)*

## Summer is Almost Over

I say to you — See the colors
changing? Green to yellow,
yellow to gold, gold to brown.

I ask — Do you know what season comes
after summer? You look away, out the window.
Fall, I tell you, the season when

leaves fall from the trees. Fall
you say softly, slowly. Will that season
always bring back memories? Leaves

raked into piles, you jumping into them
laughing, almost disappearing. Today
you are wearing your new blue watch. Blue

still your favorite color. Looking down
you tell me — It's nine o'clock! And then
only minutes later look again and announce

It's two o'clock! Not caring yet
how quickly time and seasons pass.
When I ask what season comes after

Fall you answer right away — Winter.
You remember that long, Michigan season.
But when I ask what comes after Winter,

you look out the window again, not really caring.
Why do I want to teach you the way seasons
come and go? I look where you are looking,

see now what you see — the nuthatch,
head bobbing as it plucks and eats seeds
from the feeder, the one hanging deep in the branches

of the tall pine. She cocks her head, watches us
watching her. Nuthatches. They teach their children
songs.


  *– for Colin, age 5*

# In My Time Capsule

I will put my bedroom curtains, the ones my mother made, stirring with the breeze, first day of summer vacation.

And my collection of china horse figurines, displayed on the white plank shelf my father mounted on the wall above my bed.

My diaries — the ones with a key.

And the four-leaf clover I found at recess in second grade and kept pressed in a book.

I will put my mother kneading bread in the kitchen, laughing when I ask her if it's true, what they said on the bus — bikinis cover only the most important parts.

My father, after work, siting alone in the darkening living room, listening to Mario Lanza.

My copy of *Gone with the Wind*. I stayed inside reading for three straight days, the summer we rented a cottage on Green Lake.

The night he asked me to dance.

My 128 Macintosh computer.

A roll of undeveloped Kodak film

Grandfather, whistling whole songs as we walked the worn path through his orchard.

The taste of Grandmother's buckwheat pancakes with warm maple syrup tapped from maple trees in their woods beyond the orchard.

The faux diamond tiara.

Seeing my daughter, first day of kindergarten, honey hair gathered in pig tales, waving from the bus window.

My son, at ten, running up the stairs shouting, "Mom, I sailed all by myself today!"

Soaring above the water, that pelican. It could be my father in his next life, as he promised.

My mother's last half-glass of red wine.

My daughter, tucked in bed, calling after me — "One more hug, Mommy! One more hug!"

My son, the day he left for college, surprised, tears slipping into his Frosted Flakes.

The names of all the dogs I have ever loved — Cherie, Sandy, Brie, Sophia, Daphne, Ellie.

The thud of sea waves, spray exploding against the rocks.

The names of all my grandchildren.

Photographs of him — at twenty, thirty, forty, fifty, sixty, seventy, eighty, ninety, one-hundred, he's sure he'll live that long.

Photographs of our children at one and five, ten and sixteen.

Their wedding photograph — smiling, holding hands with the one they love.

Fuchsia bougainvillea, luminous, shining through the window, the long cream drapes lifting, moving.

Our secret door through bookshelves.

The wedding ring he chose with its heart shaped diamond.

His gold band, engraved on the inside with — *Je t'aime, toujours*

This sky, clouds glowing neon pink and orange, as the sun sets over Lake Michigan

All the poems I've learned by heart.

My last poem.

# Star Light

Look over your shoulder. See again
the years when you were ten, twenty, thirty —
keep counting. See how it can be
that you are here now but began
then. And pray, or dream — it
can be the same — that whenever you
stop counting, part of you will
linger low and near,
a star in the dark.

## End Notes

**I Am Small,** *p. 1*
I heard Edward Hirsch read his poem *Special Orders* (from his book entitled *Special Orders*) on the Diane Rehm Show. His opening line "Give me back my father walking the halls" gave me back my father, walking the halls of the nursing home, wearing his WWII brimmed cap with the aircraft carrier Essex insignia. Alzheimer's was taking him from us — a sad and poignant memory. But using that opening line as a prompt I found my way back to the strong, loving father remembered in this poem.

**They Walk the Same Way,** *p. 10*
The original dedication was — *for Bob and Dominique, who believe "there is always a way."* That's the deep conviction I see in the way they both lean into the wind, into each day. And I have been grateful to them again and again for so believing.

**Write a Poem,** *p. 14*
Early one morning when we were in Mexico, my husband walked into the room where I was writing and said with great passion, "You need to write a poem about…" and then proceeded to describe to me the beautiful images he had just seen from our bedroom window. In effect he wrote this poem for me! Hence the dedication — *Gracias Roberto*. And I do thank you, Roberto, for your growing poetic sensibility and forty-four years of creating a life-long poem.

**It Could Have Been Otherwise,** *p. 15*
For a generation that one day might not know the song to which I'm referring, the title was *"When I'm Sixty-Four"*, written by Paul McCartney and released in 1967 (I was a sophomore in high school!) by the Beatles — John Lennon, Paul MCartney, George Harrison and Ringo Star.

**Fly Boy, Fly,** *p. 21*
My father, Russell H. Volkema, (1920–2001) was a Navy pilot during World War II, serving in the Pacific on board the U.S.S. Essex. Though he was a pilot and had trained pilots before being assigned to the U.S.S. Essex, he probably survived WWII because he did not fly missions but was instead utilized as a dispatcher. He saved the lives of others too, because he saw that what was then the standard way of dispatching planes — straight off the prow of the ship — made it impossible to rescue pilots who did not gain enough loft for takeoff. Believing it would be safer to dispatch planes at an angle off the side of the carrier deck, he began doing that instead. Records indicate that he was the first, in any Allied Navy, to have begun dispatching in this manner. For this he was given a Navy Medal of Honor on January 31, 2000, at the age of 79.

**Prayer of the Cockroach,** *p. 27*
This poem came to me as I watched a sleek black cockroach scuttle up a wall. A metaphor came to mind in light of the recent election of the first Black President — Barak Hussein Obama. But it is a metaphor not only for Obama but all those who struggle to survive oppressive discrimination by the powerful.

**Valentine,** *p. 33*
My Valentine to Bob, Cabo, Mexico, 2015

**This Time,** *p. 43*
It is the poem *Forgetfulness*, by former Poet Laureate Billy Collins that is alluded to in this poem. A poem, like so many of his amazing poems, making us laugh, giving us courage.

**News, Sports and Weather,** *p. 44*
It was friend and mentor Jack Ridl who said during one writing retreat, "Why News, Sports and Weather? Why not Poetry too? I mean — think what a difference that would make!" And I agree!

**There is Nothing You Can Do,** *p. 61*
This poem is dedicated to all those who have suffered loss and still survive. And to family and friends who gather round and hold us.

**Don't Just Stand There — Scream! Run!,** *p. 67*
I have collected these poems, in part I think, to do what I so longed a grandmother, who I never knew, would have done — left some record of her thoughts and feelings, in her own words.

My father's mother, Hazel Volkema, died a few months after I was born. What I know of her is only through the stories my father told. She was so very bright, he said, did well in school (he had one of her grade cards to prove it) but didn't go beyond 8th grade — which is as far as any woman was expected to go in the early 1900's. She found work in a factory where she met a boy and married him — because she had to, because she was pregnant. The wedding held not in a church but in her parent's home. There was no other name than "sin" for this in her world, at that time.

The man she married, my grandfather was full of wild plans and dreams — but every one of them failed, due in part, but only in part, to the Great Depression. One of my father's early and searing memories is watching the auctioneer sell their house, the farm, their tools, the livestock — everything they owned. And he remembers watching his parents count the total, knowing it wasn't enough to cover their debts.

But more tragic than their destitution was the birth of my father's physically and mentally disabled brother, born years before they lost the farm when my father was not quite two years old. His brother Andrew (named after my grandfather, Andrew) never spoke more than a stunted speech, never walked, never thrived. In a picture I've seen, his legs and arms were so thin that he looked like a Holocaust victim. "B" as he was called, because that was a sound he could make (letting him believe he was saying his own name) died at 14, having depleted his mother's love and care and strength. Which was the reason she'd had little left to offer my father or her other children. After his death, she grew more and more withdrawn and strange, though this may also have been symptom of what we now call early onset Alzheimer's from which she died at 57.

She haunts me, this grandmother I never knew, whose blood runs through my veins. What did she feel through those years? What made her laugh? What made her cry? Who and what did she love? I don't know. I'll never know.

### On Seeing Again — My Father's Face, *p. 69*
I was working at the computer on what I would be saying the next day, in a courtroom, testifying. My father had been a plaintiff's attorney — would have wanted to be with me as I prepared, as I testified. But he had been gone almost a decade. I heard a sudden crashing sound, knew something had fallen over downstairs, but waited until I'd finished to check what it might have been. As I walked down the stairs, I saw at the foot of the stairs a picture frame face down on the floor. When I picked it up and looked at the picture, it was the portrait of my father and mother, the one I keep on a shelf on my wall of bookshelves. It had fallen from five shelves up and wasn't close to any of the open windows where wind might have caught it. It had never happened before. I don't know how or why that one picture fell at that particular and anxious time. All I know is that I felt my father near, hoped he was near, hugged his picture to me and cried.

### Put Down Your Pack, *p. 70*
I still hear your voice Dan, on that summer morning in August, 2014, so comforting and strong saying, "It's over, all of it, over." Thank you Dan, for walking with me, for holding me above the waterline time and time again.

And attribution is due to poet William Stafford, who in his poem, "How to Regain Your Soul" gave me a title and the way in to this poem. The poem I could finally write.

### After Words, *p. 87*
And those beloved Bichons were: Sandy, inherited from Dan and Pat, our very first Bichon who made us fall in love with her breed. Then, Brie, Sophie, Daphne and now Ellie, daughter of Daphne (who was my mother's dog) turning 12 this year. Wishing Ellie many more years. And to those before her I want to say — I still feel you near.

### Morning Sky, *p. 89*
So many memories of our first grandsons Colin and Wyatt, intent and content with their crayons and a sheet of blank white paper. And Wyatt — I kept your picture of that Mexican blue morning.

### Life after Forty, *p. 91*
This poem is dedicated to my daughter, who had entered her fortied year. But it can be a hopeful image at any age. And for that image I need to thank Marchiene Rienstra, wise woman and life-long friend, for telling me of her "aha" on that morning walk in Sedona when she saw so clearly that the summit was still ahead.

### For My Son at Thirty-Two, *p. 93*
Written for Dominique and Julie as we awaited the birth of the little one they would name Jacob Robert DeNooyer — born August 7, 2012.

### The Two of You, *p. 99*
As I gather together these poems, grandsons Ethan and Alex are barely two years old. I smile, eagerly awaiting what one of them will say or do that sends a little poem skipping my way.

### "This Snow is Delicious", *p. 100*
How my grandson Jacob loved the word "delicious" using it to describe everything that delighted him. And how we delighted in his long drawn out way of saying it — "Dee-lii-cious!"

www.ingramcontent.com/pod-product-compliance
Lightning Source LLC
Chambersburg PA
CBHW070113080526
44586CB00013B/1278